Armchair Man to Ironman

by

Jonny Nelson

W0028867

ISBN: 978-1-291-56814-1

PublishNation, London

www.publishnation.co.uk

Safety pins and sympathy

Here I was thirty-eight years old with another relationship that had gone down the pan. Along with feeling really sorry for myself, I had put on a load of weight and my confidence was at an all-time low.

Six months earlier I had watched a clip of a man called Dick Hoyt, who had done the Ironman with his disabled son Rick Hoyt. I remember just being in awe of this sixty-plus man swimming and pulling his son in a dinghy then pulling Rick on his cycle and running a marathon whilst pushing him in his wheelchair. I was so inspired at how a father's love for his son would allow him to put his body through the things he puts himself through. Rick says that when he is racing he forgets about his disability and feels free. Dick always says that Rick couldn't do it without him and he wouldn't do it without Rick. Anyway, after re-inspiring myself watching videos of Dick and his son on YouTube I remember phoning my mate Tony Benson and saying, "Shall we do Ironman." He laughed down the phone and said, "Do you think we could?" Bearing in mind Benson had just overcome quite a bad drug addiction my answer was, "Why not? If Dick Hoyt can do it carrying his son then why not us just carrying ourselves."

The first run we went for was a complete washout. Benson had a stitch-from-hell after about a mile and struggled to get his breath. As for me, I could actually taste the alcohol sweating out of me from the night before and, with my beer-belly and man-boobs bouncing about all over, we decided to call it a day after about two miles.

We continued to do little bits of training as and when we could in between me trying to run my own development company, being responsible for running the sites and the lads, as well as ordering all the materials for the sites. Whilst still being hands on, doing a lot of the brickwork and plastering etc., I needed to find time in the evenings for all the paperwork side of the business, pricing/invoicing, so a lot of my time was consumed with work and being a dad to my fifteen-year-old son, Daniel. I would also have my twelve-year-old daughter, Mia Rose, who lived with her mum, visiting a couple of times a week. So I was conscious of spending the quality time with my children that they deserved. Benson was also working full-time on the roads and trying to fit in a counselling course as well. To be honest we were just playing at it. Our runs weren't really up to much and were lucky to run more than three miles, and that was on a good day. We had no idea whatsoever of what training for Ironman would entail.

I have never been the best runner as I am flat-footed and need insoles in my trainers to form an arch in my foot. So running is a bit of a strain to say the least and something I really need to work hard at. Neither of us had a bike so the cycling was out of the window. And the swimming? Well, I could only swim breaststroke and Benson could manage a couple of lengths front crawl. Our Ironman dream seemed like a million miles away.

Around Christmastime 2011 my children's mum took them for a holiday-of-a-lifetime to Australia and I wasn't looking forward to the prospect of being on my own over Christmastime. So I asked Benson if he fancied getting away over the festive period. He jumped at the chance, so it was a case of getting down to the travel agents and booking somewhere. Lanzarote, here we come!

It wasn't like any other typical lads holiday that I've been on before. It wasn't fuelled by drink and women etc. It was quite the opposite. It gave me a perfect opportunity to really reflect on life and what I wanted to do with it. We spent a lot of time running in the mornings and hiring bikes to see a bit of the island. For once, alcohol wasn't a major factor as it had been before. If I'm being honest, alcohol's been a massive demon in my life which has ruined so many things, so it was like a breath of fresh air just being over there training and having something positive to focus on.

On our return from our week in the sun I was focussed on what I needed to do and where I needed to go. I joined a triathlon club in Bolton and it just confirmed to me how much work I really had to do. I was literally being lapped around the track by nearly everybody. Although the people who ran the club were really encouraging, it was probably the state of my mind and where I was that had produced this lack of confidence, so I only went about three or four times before I gave it up.

I decided to go on the UK results website and enter myself into a race, basically just to get fit at my own pace and build my confidence up slowly. So there it was, the Chernobyl 10k in Preston. I rang Benson and asked him to book the same race. I think we had about two weeks to train for this massive gruelling six-mile race. With this in mind I thought that Ironman, with its 2.4 mile swim, the 112 mile bike ride and the 26.2 mile run, would be a doddle if we completed the Chernobyl 10k.

The two weeks leading up to this, from a personal point of view, were a bit naff. I was struggling a bit financially as, just after Christmas, nobody is interested in spending money and having building work done. I was also feeling a bit sorry for myself from the breakup of a previous relationship. Benson also pulled out of the race as he was full of the flu, so the night before the race I buckled and I hit the drink. I had been doing so good and was so focussed on the goals I had set, but circumstances just got the better of me and that was that, enough said. Sunday 29th January 2012, the day of the race, I really wasn't feeling my best. I jumped in my ford transit van with an old t-shirt on and a pair of shorts and headed off on my journey to Preston. I ended up getting lost and by the time I arrived I ended up parking quite a distance from the "meet". I went to get my number and they had no safety pins left to pin them on, so there I was, on my hands and knees, crawling round a pub trying to find safety pins and miraculously managed to find two.

I was at the start line of my first race and just laughing to myself at me in my old t-shirt and shorts and all these runners, with their proper kit on, looking the part. I felt totally out of my depth and contemplated if I should just go and get a beer from the pub where I got my number. That thought was rudely interrupted by this man blowing a whistle for the start of the race. Ignorance of some people, hey! Away we went, me with a hangover-from-hell and with the enthusiasm of, well, someone who's got no enthusiasm, and my number held on by two safety pins flapping about all over. I tried to keep up with the fast start everybody seemed to make but that soon disappeared into the slow pace I was comfortable with. I couldn't believe the people overtaking me, men and women in their seventies and overweight people, yet I was running my hardest! I was putting in maximum effort, I had items from my nose all over my face and I couldn't breathe properly. I even found myself lying to the spectators on the way round saying, "Things you do for charity, hey?" so they'd feel sorry for me, and getting responses of, "Aw, well done, he's running for charity." Anyway, I staggered in at 59:29, got my medal, jumped in my van and headed off home. I couldn't resist calling in on Benson and showing off my medal. He was gutted, he wanted a medal, he even wanted mine, under Benson's own admission he is only EVER doing it for the medals.

We continued to keep on top of the running, getting in some seven and eight mile distances with a pace that wasn't really worth writing home about. Times didn't even enter my head. I was more concerned with just getting round the distances and in one piece. We booked another run, 18th February, the Standish Hall 10k Trail Race, which was on a Saturday quite late in the afternoon about 2.30 pm. It had been raining all morning so having never done a trail race before I didn't know what to expect at all. Regardless, we travelled up there with Benson's mate Danny Hardman who was a cage fighter and was using the run as a training run for an up-and-coming fight he had. Benson was getting quite fit, as he wasn't carrying any excess weight, unlike me, who was still struggling with the weight I was carrying. I had it in my head that, because I wasn't really drinking as much anymore, albeit I was still drinking, I could replace it with chocolates, takeaways, fizzy-pop and biscuits and it not make a difference. Not a good idea! Race time came and away we went, everybody slipping and sliding all over. The conditions were not good. In fact, they were diabolical. Danny was off to a flyer, Benson not that far behind and me spraining my ankle about ten minutes into the race. I remember thinking, there is no way I'm stopping and making excuses as to why I couldn't finish.

I finished the race in 1:04:49. I was a bit disappointed as I thought I had been working hard on my running and I didn't even beat my last 10k time. Later that evening, after I had got home and had a long soak in the bath and watched my ankle swell up to double the size, I reflected on the race and thought, under the circumstances, it wasn't a bad effort. You can't really compare your times between a road race and a trail race as they are very different.

Oh and forgot to mention, Benson didn't get a medal as they weren't giving them out that day. He was gutted. He complained that much I nearly went and bought him one myself.

At this point, we were only really concentrating on our running. I think we must have forgotten that triathlon had another two disciplines and we couldn't do those either, so we decided to join a local gym. I also wanted to find an alternative to my nightly routine of watching TV and eating junk food after doing the work-related paperwork and the nightly household chores that we all have to do, cooking tea, washing and ironing etc. My son Daniel is like any other fifteen-year-old boy and wants to be out with his pals and not stuck in with his dad, so the nights were getting very tedious and boring to say the least.

Upping the pace

The gym I joined was open until ten o'clock at night so it gave me plenty of time to do what I needed to do at home then get to the gym for an hour or two. I really wanted to concentrate on building my legs up on the bike so that was my first port of call. I thought I was getting in reasonable condition because I could run seven or eight miles but being on that bike for twenty minutes soon proved me wrong. I had never seen so much sweat come out of my body in my whole life. Even my eyelids were sweating. I was under the impression that the cycling would be easy as you was sat down, but how wrong could I be? It was another shock to the system; I couldn't cycle more than 10k on the bike without struggling.

I continued to go on the bike for another couple of weeks building it up to 20k. As I had my head down cycling I started to think about Ironman and the task in hand. It dawned on me that after completing the 112 mile cycle you would have to jump off your bike and run a marathon. Right then I thought to myself, "OK, I've just cycled 20k." I made my way over to the treadmill. Well, my legs were all over the place, my breathing was the same and I looked like someone had whacked me in the face with a massive beetroot. I couldn't even run 3k... Session over! "What am I doing? Who am I trying to kid?" were the thoughts going round in my head walking past the mirror. Catching a glimpse of my fat gut, I felt like just giving up on it all. Them thoughts didn't last for long. Giving up's not an option. "C'mon, Ironman. Let's have ya."

We decided to book the Blackpool Half Marathon on Sunday 11th of March 2012 but neither me nor Benson had ever ran this sort of distance before so it was definitely unknown territory. We travelled up to Blackpool; me, Benson and another mate of mine called Lee. Lee had already signed up for Ironman Bolton 2012, so this was a training run for him. The race started outside the Hilton hotel, running up and past the pleasure beach then back to the Hilton, then running the other way and coming back on yourself. When I had ran past the pleasure beach and got back to the Hilton I really felt like just giving up. I was at the six-mile point and just felt like I had no energy at all. I carried on regardless, finishing the run in 02:20:25 and I honestly couldn't have ran another step. It was absolute agony. My legs seized up and I remember saying to Lee, "That was disgusting." But I never would have dreamed of running that distance three months prior, so very slowly but very surely I was getting there.

Lee got a time under two hours, which is what he wanted at that point of his training programme so he was pleased. I asked Benson what time he got and he didn't know. He was just stood there with this big cheesy grin wearing his medal. Anyway his time was 02:04:48. I've never seen anybody so proud of having a medal. He even wore it for work the following week. It was only when his mum told him to take it off because he looked like an idiot eating his tea with it round his neck that he did. I can truly say he'll be the worst advertisement for Ironman ever. He'll have the Ironman tattoo on his face I reckon. Occasionally when you compete in these events there are photographers taking snaps of you on the way round. Anyway this particular picture I found on the website of myself I looked quite huge, so I ordered a copy and had it printed on a mug. Every time I'm having a brew I have a look and it gives me the push I need in the times when I can't be bothered to train.

I was over the moon at completing a half marathon distance and I was happy with the running progress. Even though the times were slow I knew that would come in time, so it was now a case of turning my attention to one of the other disciplines Ironman required, the swim. I could only swim breaststroke and had never done front crawl in my life. Front crawl was the stroke I needed so I enquired about swimming lessons at the gym that I had recently become a member of. They were working out quite expensive as you had to book a minimum of four lessons, working out at £80, but the gym said it would be possible for me and Benson to book two lessons each and split the cost, so £40 wasn't too painful to our pockets. Our first lesson was at quarter to eight on a Monday with a chap called Justin. Firstly he asked to have a look at what we could do so he could see the level we was capable of and build from that. Anyway, I was useless. In fact I was worse than useless with my arms all over the show and my legs even worse. I only swam about half a length and I felt like my heart was going to jump out of my chest. But Benson was a natural making it look so easy and then the usual doubts started to enter my head again as to what I was doing. When the forty-five minute lesson was over I decided to go and have a sauna. I felt totally off-balance and on entering the sauna I staggered into somebody trying to get up on the bench. Getting out of the sauna and still off balance I slipped right on my arse in front of about five people. If this is what it was like after a basic swimming lesson what was it going to be like getting out of open water having done 2.4 miles? I couldn't get out of the gym fast enough that day. But the following week the lesson went a little bit better. I wasn't sniffing all the water up like I was the previous week and managed to swim a full length without drinking the contents of the pool. After the lesson Benson was pretty competent and only had his swim fitness to work on whereas for me it was evident that lots more lessons where needed.

Meanwhile, we did the Salford 10k. It was a bank holiday, Friday 6th April 2012. I started to think for the first time about timings and to start picking up my pace and running out of my comfort zone. I wanted to beat my last 10k road race time, the Chernobyl 10k, when I got a time of 59:29. I wasn't bothered if I only beat it by seconds. I just wanted to beat it. So, away we went. I started off at my own pace and didn't worry about what anybody else was doing. I felt really comfortable even though I felt I put a lot more effort in than previous races and got a time of 51:14, a great result and a real indication that I was making progress. Benson got a time of 51:00, which at first I thought, great, I was only fourteen seconds behind him, until he told me that his knee had popped out of place halfway round. He was gutted and after seeing the doctor the following week he was told he would need to have an operation as it was an old injury from a previous occasion. He rang me devastated, as he felt all the training he had done had been for nothing. I assured him that the beauty of Ironman was that he had another two disciplines he could concentrate on. "The block of granite which was an obstacle in the pathway of the weak becomes a stepping-stone in the pathway of the strong." (Thomas Carlyle).

I must admit I felt a little demotivated myself at this point with my training partner being injured, also work was busy and I was conscious about spending a bit of time with my children. The Easter holidays were just around the corner so I booked a caravan for the weekend at Marton Mere in Blackpool. We had a great time and it just got me thinking about life in general. Previously I knew I was guilty of spending far too much time concentrating on what I hadn't got instead of focussing on what I had got. I felt so lucky to have my two amazing children and my health and also my ability to chase my dream of Ironman. On the holiday I remember Benson ringing to tell me that his all-singing, all-dancing triathlon bike had arrived and that he'd just cycled seventeen miles on his first outing. He then went on to say that whoever invented saddles wanted shooting. Benson paid about £1600 for his bike as he'd been saving for a while. I had nowhere near that kind of money, not for a bike anyway, so I was still looking on good old eBay hoping it would come up trumps.

After the weekend away and batteries recharged I was itching to start training again. I went out and did a twelve-mile run and felt really good doing it which gave me a confidence boost as I had the Fleetwood 10 Mile coming up on the 29th of April.

It turned out that Benson didn't need an operation on his knee after all. He just needed physio treatment and strengthening workouts, so I rang him the night before the Fleetwood 10 Mile to see if he was up for it. He wasn't, but then went on to say that one of the other lads could take his place as it had been paid for and he wanted the medal. He was deadly serious. I said he was only in it for the medals.

The morning of the race I looked out of the window and it was absolutely hammering down and blowing a gale. What I am doing? I must be mad, I thought. No c'mon, Jonny, nothing worthwhile comes easy. I started to get my gear together. My mum and her partner was giving me a lift as my two children wanted to come as well. When we arrived I was on the minutes again. I went to collect my number and there had been some cockup with the online payment so they wanted £16 off me. I didn't have it on me as I didn't think to bring any money. I went back out to the car park to borrow some money off my mum or her partner. As Mark pulled a fiver out of his pocket a gust of wind blew it straight out of his hand, so here we were chasing a £5 note round the YMCA car park in Fleetwood ten minutes before the race. Bloody typical.

With the weather conditions and being on the seafront I would have been pleased with a time around the 1hr 45 point. So I said to my mum, as she wanted to take my kids to the arcade, to come back in an hour and three quarters to see me finish. Anyway I got a time better than anticipated, finishing in 1:32:55. I expected to come in to the loud roars of my cheering fan club but they were nowhere to be seen. My kids had been starving and mithered my mum to take them for chips.

I booked another four swimming lessons and, although I was swimming about ten lengths front crawl, I was still stopping between each length. I just couldn't seem to control my breathing. My swimming instructor said in a few weeks' time, if I kept plugging away at it, the breathing issues would be a thing of the past. Bloody hope so, I thought, what if I'm in open water and I'm feeling like this? There are no sides of the pool to grab on to.

The gym also did a spin class on a Thursday evening which was free as part of the gym membership. I knew some of the guys went, who were training for the 2012 Ironman. So, if it was good enough for them it was good enough for me. The instructors there really made you work and if you didn't have enough resistance on your bike they would find you out and would tell you, in front of the class, that you weren't working hard enough. Really enjoyable though and I would recommend it to anyone as they push you that little bit more.

I also did the Bupa Great Manchester Run on the 20th May 2012. I wanted to raise some money for The Christie charity as cancer is a cruel disease and I have lost loved ones myself through this illness. My time wasn't great at 57:00 and I felt I had no energy all the way round, but I wasn't going to be too hard on myself as it was a great event where the crowds were brilliant. I got round it and I raised some decent money for Christies so happy days.

I'd just like to add that, going back to the previous run, yes it did enter my head that I should have been flying round as I had done longer distances previously. So, why did I feel so tired? These things happen. It could be the fact that you had done too much through the week or, in my case, work commitments had taken their toll. Listen to your body and if you need a couple of days off then have them. It won't do you any harm. Rest and recovery are so important. I was guilty of being really hard on myself if I missed a training session, like I was failing. You're not failing at all. We are only human and getting yourself in shape is a progression which can't be done overnight.

Finally, I managed to get some money together for my Bike. It was a Viking San Remo and it cost me £350. We would all like to go out and pay £2000 for a state-of-the-art, carbon-fibre bike, but the main thing, when you're starting off, is getting out there on a bike and building up the muscles on those biking legs. My first outing was just a case of getting used to the bike, learning the gears and generally getting a feel for my new best friend.

Meanwhile, going back to the swimming, I had got to a stage now where I could do two lengths without having to take a break. I was doing this about ten times, averaging twenty lengths, so it does come with plenty of practice. There is a load of advice also on the internet on perfecting your stroke. Being quite tall at 5ft 11, I just kept working on trying to get full reach and keeping long. I also got a float to put between my ankles and do a few lengths using my arms only as I found that my legs were all over the place and I wasn't keeping them together and paddling properly. I was told by my instructor that it was like I was pulling a parachute while I was swimming. I certainly wasn't enjoying swimming and learning this new stroke. There was just so many things to work on and think about; keeping my legs straight, kicking from the hips, pointing my toes, keeping my arms straight and streamline, my head position correct and if this didn't give me enough to think about I also had to breathe, oh and find some decent goggles that didn't leak in one eye every time I got in the pool. In total I had ten swimming lessons and felt ok in my abilities that I could progress by myself. I knew the things that needed to be worked on.

Standish Hall Trail Race - 18th February 2012 - I didn't realise that a road race and a trail race could be so different, struggling on this picture carrying the excess weight.

Enjoying some quality time with my children on holiday at Marton Mere, Lancashire.

Bupa Great Manchester Run - 20th May 2012 - I ran for the Christie charity and wanted to raise money as I had lost loved ones to this disease.

Fleetwood, Fylde Coast - 29th April 2012. It was blowing a gale that day and didn't help being on the seafront.

Ache's pains and open waters

I had a few weeks' layoff as I was just feeling a bit flat and demotivated and the whole idea of pursuing this goal was to enjoy the journey as well, so if I ever got to a stage where the training felt like a massive chore then I was going to take time out to recharge myself.

I got back to it by booking the Windmill Half Marathon in Lytham St Annes on the 15th July 2012. I thought, what the hell I've done the distance before I can do it again. I turned up and there was just loads of people with running club vests on. Don't get me wrong, it can be a bit intimidating but, as I said previously, it's all about running your own race.

I decided that I was going to start taking the gels on my runs to start getting used to eating and drinking whilst being on the go. So there I was at the start line and I decided to have a gel before the race kicked off. As I opened it with my teeth it went flying all over the guy in front landing all over his hand. I swiftly moved to one side watching the fella look up at the sky. I think he thought one of the local seagulls had shite all over him as he was looking round in disgust.

The race went ok. I got a time of 2:17:03, beating my time of the Blackpool Half Marathon by just over three minutes, so I was pretty pleased with that.

I went to support my mate Lee Smith do Ironman UK on the 22nd of July 2012 in Bolton which was very handy as it's my home town, so I knew all the best places to go and spectate. I advise anyone thinking of doing an Ironman to go and watch it first, as the buzz it gives you, especially if you know somebody competing, is absolutely awesome. Lee did really well for his first time at this distance and watching him complete it just confirmed to me even more that I wanted to do this event.

I spoke to Lee the following day and he said he had learned a couple of brutal lessons, one being that he should have worn sun cream and also that he wished he had done more brick sessions. (Brick sessions are combining the disciplines together.) He said where he would go and cycle fifty miles come home and be pleased with that, what he should have done, by his own admission, was cycle the fifty miles then go out and do a ten mile run, which he didn't do. So with this advice, I started off by going out cycling five miles then running three miles then back on my bike and cycling another five miles, just to get my legs used to running after getting off the bike and with the aim of upping the distances as I got stronger and fitter. The more you can get out on the bike the better as just getting used to things like the saddle hurting your arse and the stiffness in your back and your shoulders are not an enjoyable experience either. My pedals on my bike were the stirrup type and for me weren't too comfortable but I know some people prefer them. Not me. The next thing I needed to save up for was some cleats and pedals. (Cleats are clip-on shoes, which clip on to the pedals.) With cleats you can also pull up your pedal, as opposed to just pushing, giving you the ability to cover more ground. At this point of our training we were doing the bigger bike rides on Sunday afternoons probably averaging about thirty to thirty-five miles. I also recommend getting some cycling glasses and not making the mistake I did, thinking you don't need them. The crap and flies that decide to introduce themselves to your eyes is unreal believe me.

It was time to conquer my fears and just go and do what I had been putting off for weeks. Open water swimming, what a shock. My swimming instructor, Justin, said he would take us to a local lake that he used when he was training for the channel swim. It was owned by United Utilities so we wasn't really allowed in. He had only been kicked out a handful of times, so it was fine he went on to say. We met about seven o'clock one August evening, got on our wetsuits, goggles and swim caps, and in we went. When I said what a shock I meant, what a shock! I couldn't believe how cold the water was, taking my breath away and causing me to panic big-time. Once I started to get used to the water I settled in doing a few strokes but having my face in the water and it being so cold I remember shouting to Justin, "How am I supposed to breathe?" "Same way as you do in the pool," he replied. Once I had got used to having my face in the black waters and feeling the buoyancy of the wetsuit I really started to relax and enjoy it. Benson again was a natural as he'd done loads of surfing in the past so he was away. For me I knew that open water swimming was another mountain I needed to climb, but one I was determined to conquer. Now that I was doing the three disciplines it was just a case of putting them all together and doing it well. At this point in my training it started to feel real. I wanted to be an Ironman finisher so bad that I decided I was going to live and breathe training for this event for the next year.

The running was really coming together and my pace was getting there too. We did the Fleetwood Half Marathon on the 26th August 2012. I felt strong all the way round but felt I was holding back a bit in fear of burning myself out. I beat my previous half marathon time by just over 19 minutes getting a time of 1:58:07. It was my first sub-2hr so I was chuffed as I really am not a good runner. But with a bit of grit and perseverance I was getting there, and when you do start seeing the results it does motivate you to want to do better every time. I even beat Benson in this race for the first time ever. But he had just come back from being ill (so he said) and he got a nice medal so he wasn't too disappointed.

Triathlon Time

My first triathlon was a sprint triathlon in Nantwich, Cheshire on Sunday 2nd September 2012. I phoned Benson four days previous to this event like a kid on Christmas Day saying, "I've just found this event on the net, there's spaces left, shall we book it?" Bearing in mind we had done the Fleetwood Half Marathon on the Sunday just gone. There was a silence at the other end of the phone. "Erm, is it not to soon?" was his reply. "Nah, it's a good one for beginners. Let's just get it done." So that was it, all booked and paid for. We put the bikes in my works van, dodging the cement mixers and everything else you get in a builder's van, and headed to Nantwich. Lee Smith came along for the ride as he had done the event a couple of times before. I was really grateful for this as me and Benson didn't have a clue what we were doing, which was evident by the daft questions Benson was asking like, "Do we wear our underpants?" and not forgetting, "Do we get a medal?"

It was a really well organised event and absolutely perfect for beginners. The swim was in an outdoor pool where you did sixteen lengths, four lengths in each lane. The swim went ok but, having watched a video my daughter recorded on her phone, I still had quite a bit of work on technique to do. I wasn't worried as I knew all about that. It just confirmed how bad I was. Bloody video phones have a lot to answer for.

Getting out of the water and running round to your bike transition is an experience in itself. From my point of view I was really dizzy and felt like I had no legs. At the bike transition I took off my swimming shorts and put on my cycling shorts the wrong way round. I was panicking, as I wanted to be as good as I could. I remember saying to myself, "Calm down, Jonny, relax. It's your first triathlon and you can work on times later." The bike was a twelve-mile ride. I couldn't believe how easy and comfortable the bike went. I thought afterwards that I should have put more effort into it, but it's all about knowing your own pace. That will only come from experience.

Getting off the bike and running was something else I knew I was going to have to work on. As for my legs, I felt like I had none. The run was 5k consisting of four laps round the track. It definitely took the first lap to get used to running.

Overall it was an amazing event for my first triathlon getting a time of 1:38:04, Benson also having a good result at 1:28:53.

So that was it. If I didn't have it before I had it now. The triathlon bug had well and truly bit me and I was straight on the computer looking for my next event, which so happened was a week later at Tatton Park, also in Cheshire. They had a sprint distance event on the Saturday and an Olympic distance on the Sunday. I was seriously thinking of booking the Olympic but I don't know if I was getting a bit giddy. It was an open water swim and, not having a lot of experience in open water, it may have been a bit ambitious for a second triathlon. So I booked another sprint distance for Saturday 8th September. Benson picked me up at 4.30 in the morning as registration was open from 5.30 and because we booked it last minute we didn't know what waves we was in or anything. This time we bundled our bikes in the back of Benson's little Peugeot hatchback and made our way to Tatton Park. It was a bit of a trek from the car park to the registration point and it was pretty comical trying to ride our bikes with all our gear in tow.

Once we was all set up in the transition area and had listened to the briefing we could relax and go and watch the first few waves. We was about seventh so by the time it got to the fourth wave the nerves started to kick in a bit. It wasn't the nerves of the event, again it was just swimming open water with other people for the first time. Anyway it was our time to shine. People had told me about swimming open water and about everybody scrambling over you to get past. I must have swallowed half the water in that lake that day. I was nearly choking and had to turn on my back for a minute. Once the initial rush was past, I settled in near the back with some of the people doing breaststroke. In fact some of the breaststrokers were swimming faster than me and I was doing front crawl. Anyway I did the 750 meter swim in 17:30 the cycle in 41:05 and the run in 29:46 giving me a time overall of 1:34:27, another one in the bag.

A couple of days later I got a phone call from Lee Smith. Bolton have got Ironman again 2013. Am I ready? Can I be ready? I was thinking, sod it, Bolton's my hometown and they might not get it again. So that night on the 12th of September I booked it, 4th of August 2013. I had eleven months to get myself in the best condition of my life. Benson booked it on the same night so that was it, we was committed, no going back.

It was a bit of a bonus that it was in Bolton as I could go and familiarise myself with the routes. I had booked a week off work so on the Monday I decided I was going to go and do one lap of the Ironman loop of the cycle course which loops round three times. What a complete disaster that was. I took a wrong turn in Eccleston, Bradley Wiggins territory, and ended up doing about fifty mile, as opposed to the thirty-five mile I anticipated. I kept having to get off my bike as my arse was absolutely killing me. I also went over my handlebars as I tried to get up a kerb only to realise that the strength in my arms was non-existent. My hand was pissing blood all over and by the time I eventually got home I just wanted to launch my bike as far away from me as I could. Oh well, onwards and upwards.

September was also one of the wettest I had ever known and by the time I was home from work and had done my nightly chores, getting out on my bike was a bit difficult. I decided to invest in a turbo trainer. This attaches to your bike lifting the rear wheel up slightly where it runs on a roller giving you the choice to add on or take off resistance. The first session on the turbo trainer I dropped my bike in to the highest gear and pedalled for about half an hour. Wow, what a work out. I felt like I had done about twenty mile on the road. I also found it better than the spin class as you are also getting used to your own bike, saddle etc. Turbo trainers can be a bit boring so I made sure I had a TV to watch or cranked my music up to ease the boredom, but definitely a well-recommended piece of kit. Living in England and being ruled by the weather/dark nights etc., it was a sound investment. Also to break up the monotony of the long runs I invested in a 20lb weight vest which I would run, from the witches brew car park at Rivington in Bolton, up to the top of Rivington Pike, running up what I call the devil's steps. When you get to the top of them you then run down the hill at the back, loop round and do it all over again as many times as you can. At this point of my training I managed just the once but you could certainly feel the difference in your legs and heart rate and it just seemed to make road running that little bit easier. I did the Swinton 10 Mile on the 30th September 2012, getting a time of 1:29:30 beating my last ten-miler by three minutes. My last run of 2012, and also just to break up the monotony of swim-bike-run, was HellRunner Hell Up North at Delamere Forest Park in Cheshire. About five of us went up to do it. What a fantastic event. I have never laughed so much on a race. They didn't have any mile markers. They just reckon it's between twelve and fourteen miles. Getting covered from head to toe in mud and wading through the freezing cold waters on a cold November morning was just brilliant. Loved it. I wasn't even bothered about getting a decent time as I spent the majority of the time queuing in these bogs of doom, watching people getting pulled out and being wrapped in foil because they'd got hypothermia. It took me 2:55:39 to get round but definitely the most enjoyable three hours on a run I had ever spent.

Nantwich Sprint Triathalon - 2nd September 2012 - Loading up our bikes in the back of my works van.

Nantwich Sprint Triathalon - 2nd September 2012 - Me, Benson and my son Daniel, just before the race began.

Nantwich Sprint Triathalon - 2nd September 2012 - 16 lengths in the pool felt like I was swimming the channel.

Nantwich Sprint Triathalon - 2nd September 2012 - putting my shorts on.......back to front!

Nantwich Sprint Triathalon - 2nd September 2012 - celebrating at the finish line with my daughter Mia Rose.

Tatton Park Triathalon - 8th September 2012 - Flying on my Viking San Remo, my first bike!

3 November 2012 - This was a fantastic novelty event, 12 miles of hills and bogs of doom.

Solid Structure

I felt that my training was going ok but there was no solid structure to it. I needed a training plan. I got chatting to a guy at the gym called Eric who had done Ironman Bolton 2012 and he offered to put me and Benson a training plan together. He did us a thirty-six week plan so Monday the 19th November we started it. Some people say that a thirty-six week plan may be a bit too long as you may peak too early. But it's what suits you as an individual and the amount of time that you want to put in to it and, training being my social life at the moment, I was prepared to put the time and effort in. Some of the swim drills consisted of holding a kickboard and doing 4 x 25 metre lengths. It was then when I realised, from the way I was at a complete standstill in the water paddling my legs like my life depended on it and not moving at all, that I had no kick whatsoever. My ankles were just too stiff so I kept trying to kick with breaststroke legs to push off then kick my legs. We also did a lot of one-armed strokes, holding one arm in front and just using the other then alternating it. There is not really much you can do to prepare yourself for the fifteen hundred people all scrambling over each other for the start of the Ironman swim, so I did a few drills with a guy called Ian who had also done Ironman Bolton 2012. I would swim and he would swim behind grabbing my ankles then getting at the side and pushing and shoving each other a bit. It is definitely a recommended drill, getting a few of you together and pushing/shoving each other, as it does prepare you mentally to get ready for the swim start.

Weeks 4 5 and 6 of my training plan were pretty much non-existent. I had developed athlete's foot, which can be caused from not drying your feet properly after swimming, causing my toe on my left foot to balloon right up. It was painful doing any of the training programme. I also felt a bit run down with a cold or man flu as we liked to call it. It was also Christmastime and with so much good food flying about I decided to just take the three weeks out, recharge my batteries and also get my foot totally right. "Tis the season to be jolly, tra la la la la lala la la."

It's funny how when you are doing a training programme/plan etc. you don't really account for any injuries. You just expect to sail through without any problems. I know that I certainly did. The three weeks I didn't train I managed to put a stone in weight back on because for me personally food is my weakness. I just love it, all foods, and I know that if I didn't have a manual job and I didn't train then I would be the size of a house; a big house, a big detached house with an extension. I truly believe it's not the getting fit that's difficult it's the staying fit that so many of us struggle with and I think once you get into the mentality that training isn't a chore and that it's just a way of life then that's half the battle.

My first run back was painful, only about three miles, but the human body is an amazing piece of kit that will allow your muscle memory to remember that you have been here before. So I knew it was just a case of getting through Week 7 then I would be back to where I left off giving me a good thirty weeks to get stuck in.

It seemed that every time I went out on my bike I got a puncture or when I came to a standstill I'd fall off because I forgot I had my cleats on. It became a bit of a standing joke between me and Benson. I must be the only person in history to get a puncture on my turbo trainer. Don't ask me how it happened but it did. I decided to invest in the 90% puncture-proof tyres. Apparently they slow you down slightly, but hey, I'm never going to win Ironman and, with the length of time it was taking me to change a puncture, this seemed the obvious choice. If anybody was watching us trying to change a puncture they would have died laughing. We were clueless. Benson was even going on YouTube on his phone to see how you repair a puncture and I think I caused more punctures myself by stabbing the inner tubes with the tyre leavers. I bet there's more inner tubes lying on the grass verges of Belmont than there is in a Halfords store room. I can safely say that I'm a lot better now as I've had loads of practice. Oh, and for the residents of Belmont, my apologies for not recycling and taking my inner tubes with me but my head was not in a good place at the time, sorry.

My first competitive run of 2013 was the 24th Great North West Half Marathon in Blackpool, on the 24th of February. It was a flat course so there was plenty of opportunity to get a PB (personal best). Not this time for me anyway. It felt like we had been running forever when hitting the two-mile point. Benson pipes up, "F......, two miles, is that it!" Anyway, I think I spent the next two miles just laughing at Benson at how knackered he was. It was a decent run and we both got through it, Benson getting a time of 2:00:28 beating his PB by about four minutes and myself getting a time of 1:59:46 falling short of my PB by about a minute and forty seconds. But hey, it was the first one back so I could live with that. I really needed to get some decent distances in my legs as anything over the ten-mile point I was having all sorts of aches and pains, especially in my lower back. So I continued to keep upping the distance, a mile at a time, as I had the Trimpell 20 Mile in Lancaster booked a couple of weeks later and a full marathon a few weeks after that, so I needed to get my arse in gear.

Sunday morning 17th March 2013 Benson came to pick me up. He was gutted that I was up as it was the day of the Trimpell 20 Mile. How quick that had come around? He said he was hoping I was still in bed so he could go home and pretend we had done it. We travelled to Lancaster cranking the music in the car right up to get motivated. Once we got there and registered we was sat in the car pinning our numbers and putting our energy gels into our tri-belts. I remember saying that this is becoming a regular occurrence, sitting in the car on early Sunday mornings shoving bananas down our necks and energy drinks, stinking of deep heat, oh and Benson toking on his electric cig. We must have looked like proper hard-core athletes to anyone walking past seeing a car full of smoke. We was just reflecting on the journey we had come on so far, from that first initial run where we struggled to run a couple of miles to just getting ready to run twenty miles, the longest distance we had done so far.

Again times on the bigger distance events were not that important. We just wanted to complete the distance without having to walk. We started off quite well, getting our ten-mile split time in 1:37:30, then it was all downhill from there. After thirteen miles my legs and my back was just cramping up big-time. People who run marathons go on about hitting this wall. I think I hit a wall, a fence, a gate and another wall on the other side of the gate just to piss me off. But I did what I set out to do. I got round it without walking, getting a time of 3:37:45 and Benson getting a time of 3:40:07.

I also wondered why everyone seemed to be passing us as on past races I have managed to pick people off in the latter stages of the run. But it turned out that this particular race was the road race championships, so it was evident we was part of a selected few who were new to this distance. I personally am not bothered about mementos after a race but Benson kicked off big-time saying he wanted a medal as he had just ran twenty miles of pure hell for a lousy t-shirt. I don't think he uttered a word on the way home. Oh yes he did, he said why did they advertise a medal to all finishers when you don't even get one? That's false advertising.

I couldn't believe how quick 2013 was going. It seemed to be flying by, as we was well into March and we was still having major cold snaps. The heavy snow was still making an appearance so getting out on my bike was proving to be a bit difficult. There is only so much turbo trainer you can handle so I was hoping for some decent weather soon. I was conscious that the cycle was a major part of Ironman and I had done nowhere near enough. Also, both me and Benson work outdoors. Getting in from work when you are cold to the bones it is so hard to convince yourself to get on your running gear and hit them roads. I questioned my sanity so many times during this period. But if Ironman was easy everybody would be doing it, wouldn't they?

I had a full marathon coming up next and, thinking back to the Trimpell 20, I thought that I couldn't have run another step after I had completed the twenty miles. But, thinking back over previous races, I also thought that about the half marathons. So I do believe, nine times out of ten, that it is a conscience battle. I had spoken to a few people who had done Ironman and several had said they had never run a full marathon before Ironman. But for me personally it was more psychological. If I knew I had done the distances before then I knew I could do them again.

A couple of days before the Blackpool Marathon we was out cycling and Benson was saying that there was something seriously wrong with his lower back. He said it hadn't been right since the Trimpell 20 and that he needed to get it checked out. It probably didn't help the fact that he was on a block paving contract for the council bending over day in day out.

It turned out that he had sciatica and was told to take it easy as well as having some physio treatment. He was fed up to say the least but, as I have said before and I will say it again, the whole idea of this journey to doing Ironman was to enjoy the ride and to do it within our capabilities. Ironman isn't going anywhere. It's always going to be there so whether you do it this year, next year or in ten years' time it doesn't matter.

Benson pulled out of the Blackpool Marathon and I was seriously debating about pulling out myself as I had only done a couple of small runs since the Trimpell 20 which was about 3 weeks previous. But, as stubborn as always, I rang a guy who I knew from the gym called Phil who I knew was going there with his girlfriend to do the half marathon, so I asked him if I could cadge a lift. It's always good to catch up with Phil as he has done a few half Ironmen and Ironman Wales and also doing Bolton 2013, so he always gave me some good advice. Phil was also one of the first people I met at Bolton tri club at the initial start of this journey when I was carrying loads of weight and being lapped round the track. He used to say that I'm half the man I used to be when I would see him at the gym as the weight was dropping off me bit by bit.

Anyway we arrived at Blackpool football ground and I went to pick up my number and do the familiar routine of getting ready, pin my number to tri-belt, put gels in tri-belt, attach chip-timer to trainers, put my MP3 player in my shorts pocket. One thing I made sure of this time was to put some plasters over my nipples. Having man-boobs and with the friction of them rubbing on my white top, the last time I raced it looked like I had been shot twice in the chest.

The race started and off we went. I just took my time and felt good. It got to the half marathon point and I felt great, my time being around the two hour mark. Mile 15, mile 18, mile 20 felt great. I was even ten minutes under my last twenty-mile time. Mile 21 not bad, a few twinges, but then mile 22 it was game over. I think my left and right leg was having a competition between themselves who could cramp up the most, or who could make me walk the funniest as they just wouldn't let me run. I ended up walking for five minutes then running for five minutes right up until mile 25 where it managed to ease and I could run the last mile. I got a time of 4:53:55 which is the biggest distance I was ever going to run so now it was just a case of learning to run it well.

Triathlon season had started up again so I thought I would start off where I finished last season and book a sprint tri. I entered the Pendle Triathlon on the 21st April 2013. It was in a place called Barnoldswick so I knew it would be hilly as there is a lot of them round that part of the country. I felt quite strong over the whole event and thought that I was doing ok, but my time told me something different. I was about thirteen minutes slower than I was last season when I did Tatton Park. I seemed to be overtaking a few people on the bike but a lot of them was on mountain bikes so I was probably taking it too easy, thinking that I was going faster than I was. I know that I'm a plodder in all the events and I am never going to break any records, but I was a bit frustrated after this event as I wanted to do better and I knew I could do better than this. My mentality towards competing was definitely changing. I wasn't satisfied any more with just getting round the course. I wanted to get round in times that were better than they were.

With Pendle still in my mind I decided to start to cycle to work as we had a contract in Salford, which was about twenty miles there and back from my house. I thought I would use these sessions to build up my speed and then do the bigger distances at the weekends. A lot of the lads on site thought that I wasn't right in the head as the day's work tired them out enough, but I knew this was what I needed to do to progress that bit further. Benson decided to pull out of Ironman as his back was causing him too many problems, but I know he will do Ironman one day without a shadow of a doubt. So it was back to training on my own, which I don't mind sometimes as you're not relying on other people. I'm a bit of a loner anyway in that respect, a bit like a one-man wolf pack so it was a case of head down and carry on.

I have never pushed any of my children to do anything. I have always just encouraged them in whatever interest they had in their lives and I believe you are definitely a product of your environment. My son had watched the journey I was on and the races I had done and seen how I was getting fitter. But he never seemed interested until one time after one of the events he turned round and said that he would like to do a small event himself. I entered us both in the Warrington 5k on the 12th May 2013. So, wanting him to have the full Jonny experience of what I had been going through, we arrived five minutes before the race was due to start. Then he decided he needed a pee so after running to the loo with him we got back just as the race was starting. He did really well as he had never ran that far and he said to me afterwards that he didn't realise 5k was that long. He has kept up his running and is working his way up to a 10k next. So watch this space, he'll be an Ironman that lad.

I thought I was getting quite reasonable on the bike until I went out a couple of times with a few of the guys who lived in my area; Russ, Chris and Ben. Chris has done Ironman Bolton for the last few years and set up a triathlon club called Team Deane. It's just amazing to watch how many people are joining up from being inspired and watching normal everyday hardworking men and women achieve the unachievable. I was definitely at a different level of fitness and on this particular day, I'm not joking, talk about being left behind. That was an understatement to say the least. They seemed to be waiting for me to catch up every ten minutes. They must have been thinking, who's brought this fella? I used to come home from these outings and just sit on the end of my bed thinking of ways to get better on the bike. But there is only one way and that's just hard work and perseverance I'm afraid.

I remember going up the infamous Sheep House Lane, which is part of the Ironman Bolton route and this old guy came flying past me like I was stood still. His bike looked like he'd just borrowed it off the set of Last of the Summer Wine or something, so to save face I shouted to him, "Fourth time up this for me, mate." It wasn't at all. It was my first time. I was just so embarrassed about being crap on the bike.

24th Great Northwest Half Marathon - 24th February 2013
- The first run of 2013.

Blackpool Marathon - 7th April 2013 - This is where my left and right legs were having cramping competitions between themselves.

Doubts, carbs and sun cream

I did start to really question myself as to whether I had done enough training. Not having ever done an event of this scale, how do you know if you have done enough training? How do you know if you have got your nutrition right? I convinced myself that I was pulling out and leaving it for another year.

I was in the gym that evening and I was telling this guy of my concerns that I didn't feel I had done enough training and was debating about pulling out. One of the guys from the gym called Nigel who was also training for Ironman overheard the conversation and asked why I was thinking of pulling out. I told him my reasons for why and he went on to tell me that he had a crappy old bike what he was doing it on, his back was knackered, and he struggled to run as he had bad knees. All of a sudden I felt like an elite athlete.

Nigel invited me to go cycling with him as there was a group of them who got together for big rides on Sundays and that I was welcome to come along. I tried to get out with whoever I could, getting more experience with cycling with other people.

On one occasion I was out with Ian and Nigel and I remember Nigel saying to me that I was quite scary to watch. What do you mean, was my reply. He said that when I was cycling the heel of my right foot looked like it was going to hit the chain every time I pedalled. When we had finished the cycle Nigel asked to have a look at my cleats. He hung them on a level wall and one was twisting one way and one the other way. I wondered why my knees were in agony every time I got off the bike. Anyway I straightened my cleats and, touch wood, I have not had a problem with my knees since.

Although the bike I had been using had been ok and served me well, it was time for an upgrade. I had been putting money away as one of the local bike shops in Bolton did a savings club. Every time I had a spare fifty quid I used to call in and pay it in. They would get different bikes in on a regular basis so I would fall in love with a different bike every time I went. I finally decided on a 2012 Ridley Orion. I couldn't believe the difference the first time I went out. It was just so much easier to ride and I felt totally comfortable. My previous bike had quite a long frame so I felt like I was over-reaching, hence having major backache after each ride.

I also had some tri-bars fitted and again it made so much difference just tucking up on the decline and hitting some decent speed.

It was about seven weeks before Ironman Bolton and if I'm being honest I was just wishing it was over and done with. The training just seemed to be long sessions all the time and it seemed like my whole weekend consisted of training then back to work on Monday. I didn't feel I was getting any time out. I wasn't seeing much of my kids either, so I made sure I booked a holiday straight after Ironman so I could spend some quality time with them, oh and also to pig out for a week and do absolutely nothing.

I was starting to really enjoy open water swimming and even though my speed wasn't up to much I was feeling comfortable. The way I was progressing I was hoping to get out of the water in round about 1hr 40mins, so if that was the case I could live with that.

I was still having a few sleepless nights over the bike. Not that I felt I couldn't cycle the distance but just not making the cut-off time as it was 10hrs 30 from the swim start to getting off the bike. I was constantly thinking that, on a worst-case scenario, if the cycle took me 8hrs, plus the swim, I still had fifty minutes spare including transitions.

We decided to do the Manchester to Blackpool Bike Ride which did my confidence the world of good. Just overtaking so many people and feeling strong doing it made all the hard work worthwhile. When you are constantly training with people who are better than yourself you don't see the progression sometimes. I was only normally used to overtaking people on mountain bikes but on this occasion I was overtaking proper cyclists too. I got there in about 3hrs 40mins and felt well in doing so. We cycled back to Bolton clocking about 109 miles; it was the first time I had cycled over the 100 miles and felt made up with getting that sort of mileage in.

It was a week before Ironman Bolton and I was confident enough now that I had done enough to get through it. Don't get me wrong, the negative thoughts still went through my mind, but I couldn't do any more now at this stage in the game so I was ready to go.

When people asked me, what sort of time are you looking to get? I would say that I wasn't bothered. It was the first time I had done an event of this scale and didn't care if it took me 16:59:59. I just wanted to complete it in under 17hrs.

It turned out that the week leading up to Ironman was a really busy week at work, and because I was going on holiday for a week, a couple of days after Ironman, I needed to get all the funds in place to cover the mortgage and other household bills whilst I was away. One of my work colleagues needed some help with a job that he had secured on a shop refurbishment which involved a lot of structural work installing large support steels etc. This was the kind of job I really didn't need to be doing a few days before Ironman. I didn't want to come this far and get an injury at work installing steels.

I ended up working until the Thursday as I was just knackered and needed to rest. I also needed to get my bike in for a service, sort out all my nutrition and get some new running shorts. So that was my plan on the Friday. It was also registration day at the Reebok Stadium. Oh and I still hadn't bought anything for my holidays like sun cream and a few bits of clothes. I'd not even thought about packing as I had a little event called Ironman to get out of the way first before I could even think of going on my jollies.

The Friday evening was the race briefing where they tell you all the do's and don'ts. Then after that it's the "pasta party" where they offer a bit of entertainment and the chance to load up on carbs. It was a cracking night and worth going. They asked all the Ironman virgins to stand up and I was surprised at how many people stood up which just goes to show how popular the sport is becoming.

On the Saturday is when you go and rack your bikes at transition 1. You also take your bags with all your cycling gear in it and pick up your timing chip. It give me chance to have a wander over and have a look at the swim course for the first time. It did look further than I thought but I had done the distances in training so I wasn't worried, well maybe slightly about the mass swim start but that's all.

I took my running gear to Transition 2 and at this point I just wanted to get home, rest up and chill out. I also went up to Iron Prayer, which was on about 6.30pm. I found that encouraging as I do have a strong faith in God.

Wakey wakey it's Ironman time

I went to bed at about ten o'clock that night with the intention of getting up about three o'clock as Nigel, Ian and Steve was picking me up at 4.20am. My idea was to get up at three, put my music on to get myself in the mood and wake me up, have a cup of coffee as I struggle to function without one and have a bowl of porridge. Oh and use the toilet as I knew the nerves would be kicking in.

Well in Jonnys world things very rarely go to plan and why change a habit of a lifetime so I'm lying in bed and here the constant banging of my back door, I look at my clock and its 4.20.

I'd worked so long for this day and only went and overslept. I jumped out of bed, ran downstairs to be greeted by Ian banging on my door, closely followed by Nigel. Apologising profusely I had Ian packing my wetsuit and goggles because I still hadn't got round to doing it, Nigel was grabbing my water out of the fridge and all I could think about was brushing my teeth. Until Ian said, "Forget your teeth, that's the least of your worries. You've got an Ironman to do." On the bright side at least I had a good kip.

We eventually got up to Pennington Flash where the swim was held and I realised I had left my water bottles in Steve's car. I wasn't functioning at all as I hadn't had my daily caffeine fix. I had not eaten apart from a dry peanut butter bagel that Nigel offered me and I threw away (sorry mate it was rank). I had also left my Vaseline and I was busting for the loo.

I needed to get with it. I ran to my bike where I had some flapjacks, threw one of them down my neck, bumped into Eric who did my training programme and his wife Vanessa who were both doing Ironman, asked him if I could have his Vaseline, ran to the changing tent, whapped as much Vaseline where I could, put my wetsuit half on, ran to the toilet, used the toilet, pulled up my wetsuit, put on my swimming cap, did some stretching. All sorted.

I bumped into my Mum and Mark and the kids as I was walking to the water and I was telling them about my good start to the morning. "That could only happen to you," my mum said. It's true I suppose. If it was all plain sailing then there would be no story I guess.

We all made our way into the water and I couldn't see the familiar faces of any people I knew so I just got in a position near the back and hoped it was a good call. The siren went to start the race and I felt I was in a decent position and wasn't getting kicked about too much. What did surprise me was how much harder it was to get my breathing into a rhythm. I don't know if it was because it was so early in the morning or the nerves and the adrenalin contributed but it took a good ten minutes or so for me to get comfortable.

It was an Australian exit where you do one lap, get out of the water, run a few meters then enter the water again for your second loop. I did the swim in 1hr 31mins, nine minutes quicker than I anticipated. I walked to the change tent as I'm never going to break any records so didn't see the point in running. I was about nine minutes in transition, ran out and grabbed my bike.

I had no water bottles and I knew it was about fourteen miles to my first transition so I settled for a gel and off I went. I was surprised at how comfortable I felt as I had never done any brick sessions from swim to bike I had only ever done bike to run and I was actually enjoying the bike considering I had been so nervous about it. Looking back I felt I could have put more effort into the bike but I was conscious about saving my legs as I still had a marathon to do. The support on the cycle route was fantastic, not only from my friends and family but from everyone who turned out to watch the event.

Getting in to Transition 2 and getting off my Bike though was a different story. I really didn't know how I was going to run a mile let alone a marathon. I proceeded into the sports hall at T2 and needed the loo. I had a good stretch out, got my running gear on, had a recovery drink and headed off to start the run. I looked at my watch and it was reading about 9hrs and 45mins, so I was thinking that if the worst came to the worst I could walk a marathon in seven hours.

I started to run and it took about twenty minutes before I could actually feel my legs. Once I started to get them moving I remember thinking that I felt great and that I could run a marathon at this pace. I came down Regent Road and seen a couple of friends who I knew which spurred me on. I then carried on to the Middlebrook Trail where you run along the riverbank. I had got to the end of the trail and all I could hear was, "Go on, Jonny Nelson." There was a few of my mates all waiting on the bridge and my son was there with his mates as well. At this point I felt a bit emotional and knew regardless of what happened I was going to finish this thing. I then headed on to Chorley New Road where you then do three loops into the town centre and back on yourself. I was looking at all these people with coloured armbands on and it felt like forever before I got my first green band.

Running round the town centre was definitely a test of your mental strength. You can actually hear people finishing and when you know you still have more loops to do, it can be soul destroying.

I was about ten miles into the run and my legs were just cramping up and forcing me to walk. It was the last thing I wanted to be doing as that's where all the spectators are and felt I had failed a bit because I wasn't running.

One of my mates came past me, Tex who I went to school with, and asked me if I was ok. I told him I was struggling a bit and he just said you've got loads of time just keep going which made me feel a bit better. It was getting a bit dark by this point and the last thing I wanted was to be handed a glow stick so I tried to get a shuffle on. Finally, I was coming into the town centre for the last time and I was half-walking/half-running and I remember this fella saying to me, "Make sure you run now, pal. Round the corner, that's where all the cameras are." So that was me, straight to the finish line to hear the words, "Jonny Nelson, YOU ARE AN IRONMAN!!!"

I finished in 15 hours 39 minutes. It was an unbelievable feeling and a life changing one for me as it restored my confidence in myself. I feel now that I can accomplish anything. I have heard people talk about Ironman blues and I can understand that. You train so hard for so long and then you have this euphoric high of finishing, then this void again, which again needs to be filled. For me Ironman and Triathlons in general were never going to be a one hit wonder. It was always going to be a way of life. So I think if you can just focus on your next event then these Ironman blues and low periods can definitely be avoided.

Sometimes reading books like this one can give you a sense of feeling that you may not be doing enough as in books all you read is the high points and the low points and there is never any mention of the in between. Well the in between for me consisted of being absolutely consumed by work, everyday household chores, personal problems and injuries to contend with and also giving your family the time they deserve. So yes my training at times took a bit of a back seat and there just weren't enough hours in the day. Some people might say that there's twenty-four hours in a day and there's always time to train. But for me, having a manual job, all the above to contend with and just simply finding the time was a struggle sometimes. During this journey I had so many personal issues and demons to face, which could fill another book. But I'm like a palm tree, deep-rooted and always stood tall, and in the high winds I was rocked a few times but I didn't fall as I refused to fall. I also agree that in life you need to be a little selfish and pursue your dream, but for me the pursuit of my dream became so intertwined that I asked myself the question did I make the dream or did the dream make me?

4th August 2013 - Running down the Middlebrook trail and meeting a wall of support from friends and family.

Ironman 2013 - 4th August 2013 - Enjoying my official photograph with my coveted 'Ironman' medal.

Races and Times

Chernobyl 10k	29/01/2012	59:29
Standish Hall 10k Trail Race	18/02/2012	1:04:49
Blackpool Half Marathon	11/03/2012	2:20:25
Salford 10k	6/04/2012	51:14
Fleetwood 10 Mile	29/04/2012	1:32:55
Bupa Great Manchester Run	20/05/2012	57:00
Windmill Half Marathon	15/07/2012	2:17:03
Fleetwood Half Marathon	26/08/2012	1:58:07
Nantwich Sprint Triathlon	2/09/2012	1:38:04
Tatton Park Sprint Triathlon	8/09/2012	1:34:27
Swinton 10 Mile	30/09/2012	1:29:30
Hell Runner Up North	2/11/2012	2:55:39
24th Great North West Half Marathon	24/2/2013	1:59:46
Trimpell 20 Mile	17/03/2013	3:37:45
Blackpool Marathon	7/04/2013	4:53:55
Pendle Triathlon	21/04/2013	1:50:35
Ironman Bolton	4/08/2013	15:39:40

Acknowledgements

I would like to thank so many people for helping me along this amazing journey. My two children, Daniel and Mia Rose, for sacrificing their time not spent with their dad, my Mum and Mark for coming and supporting me rain or shine at all the events and just being there in the good and bad times.

Thanks to my mate Tony Benson for starting this journey with me. You will get there, pal. I know you will and I will be there cheering you on like you was for me.

Thanks to Russ, Chris and Ben and the rest of the mighty Team Deane for their help and for waiting for me on the cycles, oh and the runs.

Thanks to Nigel for giving me that extra push when I needed it, Ian for all his advice on the bike and for making sure I got out of bed for Ironman. Phil Stevens for all his advice, my mate Tex for giving me that push on the run.

Thanks to Eric for the training programme and Vanessa for her motivation every time I went to the gym.

Thanks to Debbie and Tracy for helping put this book together and helping me word things properly.

Thanks to all the people who came out to support me. It made a massive difference and really does get you through it.

Most of all I need to thank God as without my strong faith I would not be where I am today, believe me.

If you are in a place like I was or you just want a challenge in your life then my advice is just do it because if I can then so can you… Just remember ANYTHING IS POSSIBLE.

Printed in Great Britain
by Amazon